MINDFUL MILLIONS

MINDFUL MILLIONS

SCARLETT NORA

CONTENTS

1. Introduction to Mindful Wealth Building — 1
2. Foundations of Mindful Investing — 5
3. Financial Literacy and Mindful Money Management — 9
4. Investing in the Future: Sustainable and Ethical I — 13
5. Mindful Entrepreneurship: Balancing Profit and Pur — 17
6. Navigating Economic Uncertainty with Mindfulness — 21
7. The Mind-Body Connection in Wealth Building — 23
8. Cultivating Abundance Mindset and Gratitude — 27
9. Building Resilience in Financial Planning — 31
10. Conclusion: The Path to Mindful Millions — 33

Copyright © 2024 by Scarlett Nora
All rights reserved. No part of this book may be reproduced in any manner whatsoever without written permission except in the case of brief quotations embodied in critical articles and reviews.
First Printing, 2024

CHAPTER 1

Introduction to Mindful Wealth Building

Many of us are focused on building wealth. We believe that developing greater levels of wealth will enhance our well-being and create a more secure future for our families. Our focus on wealth, however, often means that we are not enjoying the journey to well-being. What is worse, we are not savoring the simple treasures of everyday life. Instead, we are engaged in unending hours of toil, much of it in jobs and activities we do not enjoy. We use wealth as a way of trying to buy our way out of our despair. Unfortunately, our despair is that we do not have enough time to enjoy our lives. We hope that the solution to our unhappiness is to build more wealth. With more wealth, we hope to buy more time, more opportunities, and more enjoyable experiences. We think that this will make us happy.

Research on subjective well-being, often indicated by self-rated happiness, reveals that above a certain basic material foundation, not much more wealth is associated with greater levels of well-being. Recent data shows that increasing levels of happiness disappear with annual incomes in the range of $75,000 to $100,000. This amount of annual disposable income is considered enough to provide for basic, high survival needs. A significant proportion of the population has disposable income above this level, and, in consequence, these people may experience life similar to those billionaires we discussed earlier. The solution to this apparent paradox is not to possess more wealth. The paradox is that our focus on wealth as a way to enhance our well-being blinds us to mindset development. Our mindset is really about the relationship we share with money. This relationship starts from a young age and is influenced by socialization, experiences, and personal lifestyle. The real work is to focus our attention on this relationship.

Understanding the Intersection of Wealth and Well-being

The question then emerges whether aggregate measures regarding income, output, and other economic welfare can provide any meaningful information. If comprehensive human well-being is more than simply the sum total of consumption of goods and services, then this critical issue to consider is whether well-being or wealth is more important or influential. Because both wealth and well-being in their conceptual and theoretical contexts are not well established, we briefly survey the existing literature to define wealth and well-being in both aggregate and individual contexts or settings.

Participants of the Fourth International Conference on Gross National Happiness supported and further strengthened the premise that well-being can be evaluated through multiple means and that governments should adopt a plethora of social, economic, and political indicators that incorporate the concept of well-being into national decision-making procedures. This is because human life is more than simply opulence and material welfare.

There is currently debate, both academic and lay, considering whether the pursuit of happiness or well-being is part of the human condition and determines that societies and governments should orient their declared political and social goals to achieving a satisfied citizenry. Concentrating on some narrow set of resources or policies is ultimately too restrictive (or simplistic) for an effective and efficient policy implementation framework at the national and global levels.

A growing body of research now extends these ideas to discuss happiness from both micro and macro levels. However, at the micro level, few studies define, better understand, and develop the measures within the concept of wealth. Indeed, there has been, to date, no systematic effort to measure straightforward indicators of wealth and to evaluate their impact or contributions to happiness and thus well-being. The surge in interest among academics, researchers, policymakers, and practitioners about developing and implementing well-being programs justifies this research.

Now consider a person's wealth. Wealth is generally considered to comprise the total state of an individual's or family's possessions. Generally, wealth, as limited to personal wealth excluding the wealth of those outside an individual's direct family circle, could be used to represent a person's or family's financial standing, represented by some financial index or indicator. Alternatively, we view wealth not only as directly influencing well-being in its own right by generating both income and qualitative aspects of life but also as providing a means to increase access to goods and services and by positively contributing to the conceptual and structural subsets of well-being.

Consider a person's state of well-being or happiness. It is generally agreed that well-being, as experienced by a person, can consist of a general sense of purpose, positive feelings, balance, and self-esteem; positive relationships; or accomplishment and a sense of vitality. In a word, happiness refers to the state of satisfying both physical and mental needs.

CHAPTER 2

Foundations of Mindful Investing

Financial theory presumes that all investors subscribe to the same common sense. When investors let their guard down, or rely on psychological fringes to discuss financial phenomena, we label them behavioral. But let's think about the existence of this common sense in connection with this committee of investors. What if their members take for granted that the financial markets at their disposal deliver to them a constant stream of rational advice? Clearly there would then be no value to investigating why actors on the financial stage embark upon actuarially dubious quests. During falling markets, when risk capably fills the headlines, for this hypothesis to be valid, the readiness of rational financial expertise to contribute to the wellbeing of human society must also fall, and preferably faster than the overall indices come tumbling down. Regrettably, this outcome does not satisfactorily present itself.

This chapter lays the theoretical foundation for building wealth through mindfulness practices. We first sketch the prominent financial theories of decision making. These theories have given us a wealth of knowledge, not just by uncovering significant character flaws in investors, but also out of the necessity to adapt to the distinctive style of delivering information about uncertain future states. We emphasize this because remaining mindful under uncertainty is a recurring theme throughout this book. It then provides a rundown on current mainstream investment advice. A thread runs through this chapter, involving rewards for perceived risks, which is a cornerstone guiding users on how to build wealth through taking financially beneficial chances.

The Psychology of Wealth and Decision Making

So why do we make decisions that are wrong? Why don't we know when we make the right choice and the correct judgment? It is clear that after struggling to understand human behavior over many years, psychologists and other behavioral scientists know an abundance about human learning, performance, perception, and memory—knowledge that has the potential to help us make great financial decisions. Understanding differences between what we do and what we think helps us to overcome some of the problems that impede us in improving reasoning and mental accounting. It is crucial because if we know more about behavior, we might have a lot to say about practical solutions that might help us to improve the quality of our everyday judgments, business decisions, and social interactions.

Optimal decision-making is key to improving well-being and building wealth in uncertain times. Making good decisions is not always straightforward, however. In fact, a lot has been learned from psychology about the art and science of making good decisions. Isn't this a bit odd? Surely, you might think, decision making is an entirely rational process? After all, we all have a brain, so we should know when we've made a great decision or when we have exercised good judgment. It turns out things aren't that simple. As experiments and case studies have suggested, the decision-making process is often irrational, leading to the conclusion that we misunderstand the process of how we think. There is a wide range of reasons why this happens. Some of us base our decisions on inaccurate information, others respond to emotions on the day or make hasty judgments based on stereotypes or very distinct beliefs. If you compare what is known about human behavior, then it becomes clear that the scientific principles of human decision making and the wealthy and sophisticated people that walk across the faces of businessmen and women just don't match up.

CHAPTER 3

Financial Literacy and Mindful Money Management

and reported positive financial and positive social behaviors as virtues in wealthy individuals. Several recent studies connect extravagant spending with low levels of satisfaction in life. Associations between unsustainable spending and unsatisfactory conditions take into account high debt levels, economic crises, hyperinflationary periods, low levels of GDP growth, and conflicts. Causes of significant lapses in socio-economic welfare are indicated as the result of the neglect of individual well-being. Similarly, materialism has been examined many times and determined to harm intrinsic aspirations, personal growth, and prosocial behaviors. Its links to depression, poor mental health, and lower life satisfaction are also well-documented areas. Finally, contributing to conflicts, increasing carbon footprints, excessive political interest, and government control are considered threats to globalized materialism.

Inside my money-mindie-head, there's no end of stuff! Taxes and superannuation, insurance, and lease stuff! Mortgage and investments, budget-fuckit-to-it. What should I buy... a not-so-new netty doo or a spiffy new dress or a home just for two? The problems we face. The decisions we make... Where the horns on my head come to question and shake. Financial literacy is a domain where people search for this very particular knowledge base. defined a secondary trait where individuals acquire not only financial knowledge and increasing awareness, but the capacity to foster healthy money habits.

Budgeting and Saving Strategies

A traditional part of money management is to spend less than one makes. Regardless of income level, there are specific strategies that can help guide how money comes in versus how it is used to achieve a goal. Before practicing these strategies, first and foremost, establish the target objective, and also list what is coming and going; track it to determine where the money is coming from and where the majority of expenses are allocated. With this specific information, budget planners have the knowledge needed to create a realistic game plan for how money is allocated. Once all the information is gathered, create a feasible budget and determine how goals will be funded. Successful budgeting and saving money are performed descriptively using a narrative that offers reasonable priorities. A budget's details focus on making income and expenses work to strive toward funding specific goals, accumulating financial resources over time, and attaining specific target objectives such as lifestyle decisions.

Effective budgeting and smart saving habits are fundamental and critical steps to increasing wealth. If households do not have a budget, it is much more difficult to reach goals, and these deals are not related strictly to an increase in wealth. The importance of budgeting and saving money is certainly evident in America. Americans seem to make enough money to spend more than half a trillion dollars to charity. Some 50% of Americans are considered spendthrifts and have a tendency to use money to facilitate expediency, fulfillment, and entertainment. Unfortunately, the spendthrift lifestyle comes with a variety of consequences such as living paycheck to paycheck, allocating too much money toward entertainment, the lack of a consistent savings safety net, and the inability to achieve goals with a lack of a balanced portion of consuming versus saving. Furthermore, one-third of Americans do not contribute to a retirement fund.

CHAPTER 4

Investing in the Future: Sustainable and Ethical I

Sustainable investors use established financial research in a new way, selecting investments based on the standards for corporate responsibility and sustainability with which companies conduct their business and when identifying opportunities in the equity market. These researchers adhere to the philosophy that high levels of corporate responsibility and commitment to long-term strength translate into tangible financial results over time. Companies that can demonstrate leadership in the principles of environmental protection, respect for human rights, strong labor and community relations, and support a diverse and responsible workplace and produce superior financial results. Small, medium and large investment advisory companies evaluate the long-term risks and rewards associated with corporate responsibility and sustainability practices. The measurement is to assess the corporate environment for quantitative and qualitative investment in the stock market. This is the introduction to the continued development of long-term studies, although empirical research has seriously analyzed only some of the untimely returns on a fund typically achieve superior returns consistently over a multi-year cycle. They work with social policy through public stock market performance. Mutual fund companies pay attention to the increasing emphasis on the market investments. The option advances knowledge and comment on the employment.

Sustainable investing evolves from the past. Leaders in many cultures taught the importance of ensuring that the effects of any act taken in the present are decided with concern for the consequence on the future. Sustainable investing applies these timeless fundamental values of integrity and caring for others outside of traditional ethics to business, government, and more, as well as socially responsive mutual funds apply similar principles to investing in stocks and bonds. The desired outcome is a prosperous present and achievable future for everyone. By shifting from a focus on short-term gain to consistent, moderate growth, socially responsible investors are actively directing their capital into the economy in a way that fosters long-term financial health and the well-being of all.

Impact Investing and Socially Responsible Investment (SRI)

Impact investing is a rapidly maturing and evolving financial practice that seeks to attract another $1 trillion to the impact asset class. Investors in this domain are keen on earning a financial return while also contributing to the growth of social and environmental benefits they hope other businesses would pursue. The report presents an investment thesis encouraging consideration of deliberate, strategic portfolios that positively engage with climate solutions, poverty and job creation, health care and education, sustainably managed resources, urban development, and clean infrastructure. Data aggregated at the time of this writing by the Global Impact Investing Network (GIIN) show that an estimated $60 billion is now managed to seek investment returns while supporting transformational benefits, and future growth will approach an expected $2 trillion in assets under management.

For generations, a fundamental assumption has been that the business of investing achieves economic success irrespective of social or environmental impact. Today, there are many options available to investors looking to more purposefully align their money with mission-oriented values. These range from "negative screens" that filter out holdings associated with particular activities or undesirable corporate activities to more proactive investment options that take into account sustainability, growing global economies and whole-systems social and environmental solutions as part of the core due diligence and portfolio construction process. In the space between traditional investment strategies and philanthropy grows an exciting offering called impact investing.

CHAPTER 5

Mindful Entrepreneurship: Balancing Profit and Pur

We can build successful, meaningful businesses by recognizing the many harmonies and synergies between profit and purpose. Businesses do not have to succeed despite themselves. A flower company can provide meaningful work for many families, produce beautiful focal points for joyful celebrations, and purify the air by removing toxins. It can generate the profits needed to sustain and expand the business in the future, and profit can finance regenerative, beneficial projects that the entrepreneur feels are personally meaningful. Businesses can express their values through their behaviors in countless ways, large and small: volunteerism, hiring practices, how power and responsibility are shared and exercised, how waste is managed, how product stewardship is expressed, what products are sold and to whom, what kinds of relationships with their customers are supported and nurtured, and how they demonstrate their concern for the well-being of their employees and their employees' families. Business can also structure policies and programs that create personal value for their employees in their important roles as concerned community members, nurturing parents, and conscientious citizens.

Entrepreneurship is a high-wire act, and it is the rare entrepreneur who feels that she or he has achieved a sensible balance between making money and making a difference in the world. Although there are many upwellings of social and environmental entrepreneurship, most people with entrepreneurial aspirations are not motivated by the necessity of creating a meaningful and positive impact on the world, as such, but need to forge a connection between financial success and inner happiness and peace.

Creating a Business with Social Impact

It made sense to link results with achievement, with people achieving some level of economic wealth so they could enjoy the equitable processes society attempts to perpetuate, while at the same time addressing social and economic disadvantage by providing those within the system with the tools they presently lack. Using a business model to effect social change might seem like giving in, but managed correctly I believe it can produce the changes society attempts to encourage people to engage with. As a consequence, this business is unusual. It uses the multipliers of wealth creation in social responsibility and utilizes the resources of social entrepreneurship. It is a business developed through values and moral beliefs in an economic model. The company's creation uses social goals based around independence and decreased materialism; wanting more people to benefit from wellbeing not just the few social entrepreneurs who create the real value.

I've never had the intention of getting involved in business, and I am fully aware that many social entrepreneurs feel guilty about making a profit. But after talking with financiers like Mads Kjaer and Saul Minksy, it was hard not to be seduced by the possibilities of attracting big money from ordinary citizens at just a few percentage points and using those funds to launch a company that uses much more than profit and loss as performance indicators. Mads said 'Try to get people together with an idea of how to change life and to ease suffering and at the same time generate wealth'. I have never derived any great satisfaction from accumulating material goods, while attempting through my efforts to effect social change within the millions of disadvantaged people locked into the existing system. By concentrating on alternative indicators and playing to my strengths, I can focus resources on an idea that is worthy but probably underserved, which also has some probability of delivering a useful return.

CHAPTER 6

Navigating Economic Uncertainty with Mindfulness

Our world is changing. It's important to be able to manage personal investment vehicles but not at the sacrifice of your personal health. Uncertainty is a fact of life when it comes to finance as it ebbs and flows. "Mindful Millions: Building Wealth and Well-being in Uncertain Times" teachings are based on the fact that we all have untapped potential for emotional intelligence and the ability to cultivate that is already deep within us. In fact, the success of investment relies more on EQ than IQ. This book claims that if more people have the ability to gaze deeply into their lives, to develop a sense of presence, and the ability to reflect deeply, they would be able to increase their overall success. We can all increase the likelihood of building success and having more control of our financial future. If you can build your bank account with financially balanced advice and topped with the emotional intelligence previously underutilized.

Mindful Millions: Building Wealth and Well-being in Uncertain Times teaches individuals to invest in their future well-being using practical mindfulness methods. In this book written by meditation teacher, Louisa Weichmann, with a fellow wealth manager Brian P. Adams, they offer thoughtful financial advice combined with mindfulness to create a sound and practical financial plan rooted in meditation and helping individuals cultivate this emotional intelligence.

Coping Strategies for Financial Stress

Financial stress is related to both physical and emotional health problems. People under stress tend to make poor decisions, resulting in potential negative effects for their financial situations. The effects of financial stress can be long-lasting and not only reduce mental and physical health but can damage relationships and may reverse economic and social gains. In more extreme cases, financial stress can lead to bankruptcy, homelessness, and the well-documented rise in discrete mental health problems, such as depression. Helping families manage money and implement money-saving measures are examples of positive responses to financial stress. People who learn skills for figuring out how to cope with life's stressors will have the greatest chance of maintaining positive mental health.

Indeed, both recent and earlier global economic events have left many people feeling fearful, anxious, and quite insecure. As income trajectories move through a volatile economy and financial stress begins to mount, one may well be faced with having to make sense of and develop strategies to manage the complex and potentially toxic interplay between money, stress, and well-being. At its simplest, financial stress is a feeling of being overwhelmed with concerns of how to cover expenses or make ends meet. While money and work are not the only sources of stress, they are two significant concerns as a result of recent global economic events.

CHAPTER 7

The Mind-Body Connection in Wealth Building

Without evidence of high purpose, intent, and commitment to long-term wealth building, there will never be wealth. Wealth is the consequence of your ability to stay focused and committed while engaged in life's dramatic and sometimes traumatic ever-changing storyline: the quest for fulfillment, achievement, and a life of continuing learning, affection, and reciprocity. Everything truly is connected. Mindful millions evolve from living in and responding to such complexity. Managing wisely is to realize a deeper meaning to the complex. We must participate in life before we find true self. Your best effort is as a real human being. The struggle itself, worth living well, is good work. Such purpose yields good profits.

We have reached the heart of holistic wealth. The core of the book is devoted to understanding and building the critical connections between body and mind that are necessary prerequisites for the more mundane issues of managing money. Mind-body unity is the basis for the depth and flexibility of thought and deed demanded by the practical world of wealth management. The tasks of character development and acquiring practical wisdom - those specific components of the good life called understanding - are necessary to meet the requirements of growing good lives and more meaningful relationships - the broader components of the good life.

Holistic Approaches to Financial Wellness

Other holistic approaches, such as integrating financial capability into existing social safety net and human services programs, such as programs that provide job training, housing, criminal justice wrap-around services, health services, college support, and substance abuse treatments for vulnerable populations, also have the potential to achieve better financial and life outcomes. Furthermore, by using pre-treatment financial interventions to improve important financial behaviors, disadvantaged individuals with depression and anxiety could be better off. In the long term, after being more economically active and changing their beliefs and anxiety, research studies have shown that these individuals are less likely to take out expensive payday loans, are more motivated to participate in their governing processes, and have higher credit scores. Evaluated in various settings and cultures, the success of financial training represents an opportunity for policymakers.

Taylor et al. (2019) argue that holistic approaches to financial wellness, which integrate money management with broader life skills such as motivation, social interactions, decision-making, inhibitory control, self-discipline, beliefs, attitudes, values, and time preferences, have the potential to improve mental, physical, and financial outcomes. Proponents of "Shape Your Life" programs (a holistic financial wellness approach) and financial coaching programs often note the positive mental health and youth development outcomes of these services, in addition to improved financial behaviors. Mindfulness, which focuses on being fully engaged in the present moment, is often used in holistic financial wellness programs to help individuals make sound financial decisions. Preliminary evidence from the United States suggests that both active and passive users score higher on a financial wellness scale and feel more financially capable than those who did not take the Center for Financial Grandness course.

CHAPTER 8

Cultivating Abundance Mindset and Gratitude

Discovering abundance The Financial Comfort Index conducted by Country Financial in 2015 showed that over half of Americans report being comfortable with their finances. How would our perception of wealth change if abundance and wealth and well-being were not defined by the material number of dollars and things but were transferred into the individual state of fulfillment? The legendary Albert Einstein formulated his vision of wealth as follows: "A calm and modest life brings more happiness than the pursuit of success combined with constant restlessness." Amartya Sen, 1998 Nobel prize laureate in economics, views wealth as members of a human capability set that can enter a variety of achievements, but also as a set of social arrangements that enables such individual enrichment. Bill Burnett and Dave Evans, authors of Designing Your Life, suggest viewing life as a bootstrap startup. They recommend questioning the initial assumptions or the culture we all were raised in, which mostly conditions us to desire more and to find our happiness in possessions and achieving ambitious goals. More and better is never meaningful or fulfilling. What really counts is the state of mind.

Key concepts Abundance is a state of mind that comes from the belief that everything is always available to us if only we learn to appreciate and nurture it. Abundance mindset, therefore, is the sustaining belief that there will always be enough of what we need or want most. On the other hand, scarcity mindset is the belief that we never have enough. Money scarcity might be just one facet of scarcity mindset.ABSLack of satisfaction with what we own and possess, constantly comparing ourselves to people who appear to have it all, and constantly longing for more and better - that is true scarcity. All these concepts are individual and relative. Scarcity and the craving for more are what differentiate poverty from simplicity. The first is involuntary, subscription-based living on a treadmill of never enough, and the other is a conscious choice to stop chasing more and to find peace and fulfillment with what we have.

"Abundance is not something we acquire. It is something we tune into." - Wayne Dyer

Practices for Cultivating Gratitude in Wealth Building

As discussed in the previous chapter, our minds do a very good job of looking out for threats, but are not nearly as effective at recognizing the good things in life. From an evolutionary perspective, we have an overemphasis on the negative for survival value. Overemphasizing the negative, however, is one of the fastest routes to unhappiness. A daily practice of writing down three good things in a gratitude journal can lead to long-term happiness. Other practices to generate further happiness include using one's signature strengths in a new way each day, savoring positive experiences, and performing acts of kindness. Combined, these exercises can lead to long-term happiness and well-being.

Gratitude practices include expressing thanks and appreciation to others and focusing on those things in life that we are fortunate to have. Taking time to recognize that which we hold as blessings keeps our own internal experience in perspective and lessens our attachment to external wealth and objects. When we feel the lack of something, we can grow into a state of want and need. An increasing number of people are developing the wisdom to see that liberation from this kind of reactivity brings an authentic kind of happiness, and practices of gratitude are central.

CHAPTER 9

Building Resilience in Financial Planning

In both public and private spheres, the entire remuneration system, the bonus structures, and allocation of equity depend on how the financial system deems it wishes to pass its largesse to the individuals who labor for it. Given these vast resources, our economic systems have almost supernatural powers to determine our relationships - both as individuals and collectively. If these are used wisely, they can reinforce the X-factor of governance and build the social systems that we will need to cope with global forces and a new human landscape. These planetary technologies will be built for healthy, cohesive, democratic societies if we understand how meaning can be incorporated into their design. It is the power of these technologies - which build a society where happiness and contentment are not only more widespread but increasingly resilient, wealth creators themselves - assist the Mindful Millions.

The learnings of the Mindful Millions will have ramifications far wider than just providing for a more enduring, balanced, and enriched life. The need for benchmarks that measure and motivate the cultivation of greater personal resilience underpins the need for institutional resilience to cope with change and our awareness of our time and the Earth's limitations. Finance is the expertise with which we seek dominion over resources, and how we care for those resources is a powerful indicator of our investment in relationships with both our present and future selves and the environment. Institutional finance requires measures of the external risks, returns, impacts, and costs of governance that it cannot yet reliably price and an ability to build alliances with the purpose of rebuilding our rainforests, empowering girls, and managing our shared resources wisely.

Adapting to Market Volatility

With the many ups and downs of the stock market these days and Friday's one-day rise coming on top of a ten percent rise over the previous three months, we are in a classic bear rally period. The economy has pushed stock prices down due to many reasons like high interest rates, a slowing economy, record debt, budget deficit, corporate debt, Middle East crisis, and a whole host of others. It makes one question why anyone would invest in the stock market. Although, I personally believe that over time, stocks are the best asset to invest in. Taking a long-term view means spreading my investment risk over the following:

1. Balancing your investment fund among all investment assets such as large, small, and international funds and stocks, along with Treasury bonds and cash equally.

2. Keeping your investment account secure with your purchase of top-quality bonds.

3. Using most of your other investment funds to buy into undervalued segments of the market.

CHAPTER 10

Conclusion: The Path to Mindful Millions

But how is this appealing vision made achievable? How will we get from the present to this desirable future? By following these etymologically simple and for many of us seemingly rudimentary 15 easy steps and precautionary tools, both you and our mindful investment community as a whole can secure important present and continuing benefits from your potentially long-term wealth-generating activities. Along the way, mainly through the thoughtful adoption of straightforward yet mainly predictable proactive behaviors aligned with the wealth-embedded life's cycle, and through the informed use of a variety of wealth management best practices developed over the span of more than twenty years of cumulative experience by collective numerous generations of knowledgeable wealth managers and applied through countless challenging life circumstances and settings.

On this journey, readers have anticipated some of our key findings about the three most important building blocks for wealth and well-being. They've also used a series of milestones to mark the distance that would take our constellation of mindful practices from being exclusively confined to the minds and hearts of a very small group of considered minority investors who've already conquered most of that distance by engaging or previously devoting significant contemplation to many of wage-earning individuals' challenges, to the minds and hearts of millions of grateful, wise, and happy mindful millionaires and occasional other exceptional persons. With profoundly simple messages, the main tenets and principles of successful wealth management are beamed to the knowledgeable minds of every mindful investor. With the realization of profoundly simple strategies and their embodiment in a constellation of not-so-simple, yet practical, forward-thinking practices, the implementation and germination of investments bearing both meaningful fruits of calculated financial wealth and calculated well-being are made manifest.

In Mindful Millions, we've taken readers on a journey from the simple truth that money does not buy happiness all on its own, to a portfolio of not-so-simple strategies that can render many wealth investors happier and wealthier as they reorient their focus back from the elusive pursuit of ever-increasing wealth to the sustainable pursuit of well-being and the meaning and motivation that investors attach to the hard-earned wealth that is either already in their hands or in their future returns or other prospective accruals. With a careful blend of developing an honest understanding about the expected wealth management challenges ahead and proposing quite feasible ways to overcome them, we've crafted an achievable journey for our intended readers from pure profit to long-term, enduring prosperity that can serve both the wealth guardians of today and the future wealth stewards of tomorrow.

Integrating Mindfulness into Wealth Building Strategies

Purpose: The aim of this chapter is to present an overview of the historical development, current context, and possible future developments of Practice-Based Studies (PBS) for branding. It identifies the diverse philosophical debates in the practice turn, linking this to the epistemological and methodological justifications for embracing PBS. A connection is made with the specific underpinning of algorithms and the wider social and political implications for this. Furthermore, PBS is aligned with a number of scholarly debates beyond the practice turn. After discussing these contextual debates, implications for branding as a focus are presented. These illuminate branding as a socially and politically charged organizing activity. The authors encourage a multidisciplinary and cross-paradigmatic approach to the development of enriched explanations as an alternative to the pervasive neoliberal paradigm. Four contributions are set out, defining branding as communicative actions. The chapter concludes by considering the dilemmas embedded within PBS for both theory and practice.

The explosion of interest in the concept and practice of mindfulness across a range of fields over the past decade has not been restricted to addressing individual challenges but has extended to the collective level. With increasing numbers of individuals who are now more financially secure and are at specific points in their careers, including an increasing awareness of the importance of integrating their inner with their outer lives, an area of focus has been on integrating mindfulness into strategies for building wealth. Mindful wealth builder programs are starting to emerge from a diverse range of inputs including in-depth research in areas as diverse as neuropsychology, management theory, and classical spiritual frameworks. Organizations in the investment and financial planning fields are also now providing access to variations of these programs, from morning meditation to apps that track wealth giving, with an overlying intention of enhancing investor contentedness and improving wider group access to wealth creating strategies. This chapter offers an introduction to the concept of mindfulness-informed wealth building and invites the reader to reflect on the influential role they may already play, or can aspire to play as they look to augment found or familial wealth. Mindfulness is heralded as an innovation in the wealth industry, albeit one that has significant and far-reaching antecedents. We propose that it can play a strategic role in constructing wealth with meaning for today and for tomorrow.

www.ingramcontent.com/pod-product-compliance
Lightning Source LLC
LaVergne TN
LVHW092101060526
838201LV00047B/1511